2. Arise, shine

shine;____ for thy light____ is come,_____ and the glo-ry of the

77 Lord is ris - en up - on thee,_____ and the glo - ry of the Lord, the glo - ry of the Lord is ris - en up-

5
84 - on thee,_____ is ris - en up - on thee._____ And the Gen - tiles shall come to thy light,_____ and

6
92 kings to the bright - ness of thy ris - ing._____ For be - hold, I cre - ate Je - ru - sa - lem___ a re - joic - ing,_____

99 ___ and her peo - ple a joy, and her peo - ple a joy, her peo - ple___ a___ joy.

Liberamente, quasi senza misura

Allegro ♩. = ♪ of preceding

107

accelerando

7 **Presto** ♩. = 152

111

117

126

JOHN RUTTER
VISIONS

SOLO VIOLIN PART

MUSIC DEPARTMENT

OXFORD
UNIVERSITY PRESS

VISIONS

JOHN RUTTER

1. Processional and prelude: Jerusalem the blessed

Andante con moto ♩ = *c.*72 (♪ = ♪ sempre)

Urbs Je - ru-sa - lem be - a - ta, Di-cta pa-cis vi - si-
O Je - ru-sa - lem the bless - ed, Vi- sion that can nev - er

- o,_____ Quae con-stru-i-tur__ in cae - lis Vi - vis ex la - pi - di-bus,
fade;_____ Built of liv-ing stones in hea - ven, There in splen-dour bright dis-played;

Et an - ge-lis__ co-ro - na-ta, Ut spon-sa-ta co - mi - te._____
Crowned in____ glo-ry____ with God's an - gels, As a roy-al bride ar - rayed.___

Por - tae__ ni - tent mar-ga - ri - tis Ad - y-tis pa-ten-ti - bus:_____
Decked with__ pearl her__ gates re - splen-dent Wide are o-pen ev - er - more;_____

Et vir - tu-te me - ri - to - rum Il - luc in-tro - du - ci-tur
By God's grace and in - ter - ces - sion Faith-ful souls may thi - ther soar.___

Om - nes__ qui ob Chri - sti no - men Hic in mun-do pre - mi - tur.
All who__ in Christ's name have suf - fered, Those who earth-ly tri - als bore.

(♩ = 72)

poco accelerando **Poco più mosso** ♩ = 80

3. Lament for Jerusalem

4. Finale: The holy city

poco rit. al fine

OXFORD
UNIVERSITY PRESS

www.oup.com

ISBN 978-0-19-351319-8

9 780193 513198